MICHIGAN RULES OF EVIDENCE
2015 Edition

Updated through January 1, 2015

Michigan Legal Publishing Ltd.
QUICK DESK REFERENCE SERIES™

© 2014, 2015 Michigan Legal Publishing Ltd.
Grand Rapids, Michigan

Academic and bulk discounts available at
www.michlp.com

No claim to copyright of any public domain works. While we make every effort to ensure this text is accurate, there is no guarantee that the rules or statutes in this publication are the latest and most up-to-date. Accordingly, this text is for educational purposes only and should not be considered legal advice.

WE WELCOME YOUR FEEDBACK: info@michlp.com

ISBN-13: 978-1505909241
ISBN-10: 1505909244

Table of Contents

MICHIGAN RULES OF EVIDENCE 1

Part I – General 1

Rule 101; Scope 1

Rule 102; Purpose 1

Rule 103; Rulings on Evidence 1

Rule 104; Preliminary Questions 2

Rule 105; Limited Admissibility 3

Rule 106; Remainder of or Related Writings or Recorded Statements 3

Part II – Judicial Notice 4

Rule 201; Judicial Notice of Adjudicative Facts 4

Rule 202; Judicial Notice of Law 5

Part III – Presumptions 6

Rule 301; Presumptions in Civil Actions and Proceedings 6

Rule 302; Presumptions in Criminal Cases 6

Part IV – Relevancy 7

Rule 401; Definition of "Relevant Evidence" 7

Rule 402; Relevant Evidence Generally Admissible; Irrelevant Evidence Inadmissible 7

Rule 403; Exclusion of Relevant Evidence on Grounds of Prejudice, Confusion, or Waste of Time 7

Rule 404; Character Evidence Not Admissible to Prove Conduct; Exceptions; Other Crimes 7

Rule 405; Methods of Proving Character 9

Rule 406 Habit; Routine Practice 10

Rule 407; Subsequent Remedial Measures 10

Rule 408; Compromise and Offers to Compromise 10

Rule 409; Payment of Medical and Similar Expenses .. 11

Rule 410; Inadmissibility of Pleas, Plea Discussions, and Related Statements 11

Rule 411; Liability Insurance 12

Part V – Privileges 13

Rule 501; Privilege; General Rule 13

Part VI – Witnesses 14

Rule 601; Witnesses; General Rule of Competency 14

Rule 602; Lack of Personal Knowledge 14

Rule 603; Oath or Affirmation 14

Rule 604; Interpreters 14

Rule 605; Competency of Judge as Witness 15

Rule 606; Competency of Juror as Witness 15

Rule 607; Who May Impeach 15

Rule 608; Evidence of Character and Conduct of Witness 16

Rule 609; Impeachment by Evidence of Conviction of Crime 16

Rule 610; Religious Beliefs or Opinions 19

Rule 611; Mode and Order of Interrogation and Presentation 19

Rule 612; Writing or Object Used to Refresh Memory 20

Rule 613; Prior Statements of Witnesses 21

Rule 614; Calling and Interrogation of Witnesses by Court 22

Rule 615; Exclusion of Witnesses 22

PART VII – Opinion and Expert Testimony 23

Rule 701; Opinion Testimony by Lay Witnesses 23

Rule 702; Testimony by Experts....................................23

Rule 703; Bases of Opinion Testimony by Experts......23

Rule 704; Opinion on Ultimate Issue............................24

Rule 705; Disclosure of Facts or Data Underlying Expert Opinion 24

Rule 706; Court-Appointed Experts 24

Part VIII – Hearsay 26

Rule 801; Hearsay; Definitions.....................................26

Rule 802; Hearsay Rule 27

Rule 803; Hearsay Exceptions; Availability of Declarant Immaterial..27

Rule 803A; Hearsay Exception; Child's Statement About Sexual Act..33

Rule 804; Hearsay Exceptions; Declarant Unavailable 34

Rule 805; Hearsay Within Hearsay...............................38

PART IX – Authentication and Identification 40

Rule 901; Requirement of Authentication or Identification..40

Rule 902; Self-Authentication 42

Rule 903; Subscribing Witness' Testimony Unnecessary 45

PART X – Contents of Writings, Recordings, and Photographs..46

Rule 1001; Contents of Writings, Recordings, and Photographs; Definitions 46

Rule 1002; Requirement of Original 47

Rule 1003; Admissibility of Duplicates 47

Rule 1004; Admissibility of Other Evidence of Contents 47

Rule 1005; Public Records 48

Rule 1006; Summaries 48

Rule 1007; Testimony or Written Admission of a Party 48

Rule 1008; Functions of Court and Jury 48

PART XI – Miscellaneous 50

Rule 1101; Applicability 50

Rule 1102; Title 51

MICHIGAN RULES OF EVIDENCE

Part I – General

Rule 101; Scope

These rules govern proceedings in the courts of this state to the extent and with the exceptions stated in Rule 1101. A statutory rule of evidence not in conflict with these rules or other rules adopted by the Supreme Court is effective until superseded by rule or decision of the Supreme Court.

Rule 102; Purpose

These rules are intended to secure fairness in administration, elimination of unjustifiable expense and delay, and promotion of growth and development of the law of evidence to the end that the truth may be ascertained and proceedings justly determined.

Rule 103; Rulings on Evidence

(a) **Effect of erroneous ruling.** Error may not be predicated upon a ruling which admits or excludes evidence unless a substantial right of the party is affected, and

  (1) *Objection.* In case the ruling is one admitting evidence, a timely objection or motion to strike appears of record, stating the specific ground of objection, if the specific ground was not apparent from the context; or

  (2) *Offer of proof.* In case the ruling is one excluding evidence, the substance of the evidence was made

known to the court by offer or was apparent from the context within which questions were asked.

Once the court makes a definitive ruling on the record admitting or excluding evidence, either at or before trial, a party need not renew an objection or offer of proof to preserve a claim of error for appeal.

(b) **Record of offer and ruling.** The court may add any other or further statement which shows the character of the evidence, the form in which it was offered, the objection made, and the ruling thereon. It may direct the making of an offer in question and answer form.

(c) **Hearing of jury.** In jury cases, proceedings shall be conducted, to the extent practicable, so as to prevent inadmissible evidence from being suggested to the jury by any means, such as making statements or offers of proof or asking questions in the hearing of the jury.

(d) **Plain error.** Nothing in this rule precludes taking notice of plain errors affecting substantial rights although they were not brought to the attention of the court.

Rule 104; Preliminary Questions

(a) **Questions of admissibility generally.** Preliminary questions concerning the qualification of a person to be a witness, the existence of a privilege, or the admissibility of evidence shall be determined by the court, subject to the provisions of subdivision (b). In making its determination it is not bound by the Rules of Evidence except those with respect to privileges.

(b) **Relevancy conditioned on fact**. When the relevancy of evidence depends upon the fulfillment of a condition of fact, the court shall admit it upon, or subject to, the introduction of evidence sufficient to support a finding of the fulfillment of the condition.

(c) **Hearing of jury**. Hearings on the admissibility of confessions shall in all cases be conducted out of the hearing of the jury. Hearings on other preliminary matters shall be so conducted when the interests of justice require, or when an accused is a witness, and so requests.

(d) **Testimony by accused**. The accused does not, by testifying upon a preliminary matter, become subject to cross-examination as to other issues in the case.

(e) **Weight and credibility**. This rule does not limit the right of a party to introduce before the jury evidence relevant to weight or credibility.

Rule 105; Limited Admissibility

When evidence which is admissible as to one party or for one purpose but not admissible as to another party or for another purpose is admitted, the court, upon request, shall restrict the evidence to its proper scope and instruct the jury accordingly.

Rule 106; Remainder of or Related Writings or Recorded Statements

When a writing or recorded statement or part thereof is introduced by a party, an adverse party may require the introduction at that time of any other part or any other writing or recorded statement which ought in fairness to be considered contemporaneously with it.

Part II – Judicial Notice

Rule 201; Judicial Notice of Adjudicative Facts

(a) **Scope of rule**. This rule governs only judicial notice of adjudicative facts, and does not preclude judicial notice of legislative facts.

(b) **Kinds of facts**. A judicially noticed fact must be one not subject to reasonable dispute in that it is either (1) generally known within the territorial jurisdiction of the trial court or (2) capable of accurate and ready determination by resort to sources whose accuracy cannot reasonably be questioned.

(c) **When discretionary**. A court may take judicial notice, whether requested or not, and may require a party to supply necessary information.

(d) **Opportunity to be heard**. A party is entitled upon timely request to an opportunity to be heard as to the propriety of taking judicial notice and the tenor of the matter noticed. In the absence of prior notification, the request may be made after judicial notice has been taken.

(e) **Time of taking notice**. Judicial notice may be taken at any stage of the proceeding.

(f) **Instructing jury**. In a civil action or proceeding, the court shall instruct the jury to accept as conclusive any fact judicially noticed. In a criminal case, the court shall instruct the jury that it may, but is not required to, accept as conclusive any fact judicially noticed.

Rule 202; Judicial Notice of Law

(a) **When discretionary.** A court may take judicial notice without request by a party of (1) the common law, constitutions, and public statutes in force in every state, territory, and jurisdiction of the United States; (2) private acts and resolutions of the Congress of the United States and of the Legislature of Michigan, and ordinances and regulations of governmental subdivisions or agencies of Michigan; and (3) the laws of foreign countries.

(b) **When conditionally mandatory.** A court shall take judicial notice of each matter specified in paragraph (a) of this rule if a party requests it and (1) furnishes the court sufficient information to enable it properly to comply with the request and (2) has given each adverse party such notice as the court may require to enable the adverse party to prepare to meet the request.

Part III – Presumptions

Rule 301; Presumptions in Civil Actions and Proceedings

In all civil actions and proceedings not otherwise provided for by statute or by these rules, a presumption imposes on the party against whom it is directed the burden of going forward with evidence to rebut or meet the presumption, but does not shift to such party the burden of proof in the sense of the risk of nonpersuasion, which remains throughout the trial upon the party on whom it was originally cast.

Rule 302; Presumptions in Criminal Cases

(a) **Scope.** In criminal cases, presumptions against an accused, recognized at common law or created by statute, including statutory provisions that certain facts are prima facie evidence of other facts or of guilt, are governed by this rule.

(b) **Instructing the jury.** Whenever the existence of a presumed fact against an accused is submitted to the jury, the court shall instruct the jury that it may, but need not, infer the existence of the presumed fact from the basic facts and that the prosecution still bears the burden of proof beyond a reasonable doubt of all the elements of the offense.

Part IV – Relevancy

Rule 401; Definition of "Relevant Evidence"

"Relevant evidence" means evidence having any tendency to make the existence of any fact that is of consequence to the determination of the action more probable or less probable than it would be without the evidence.

Rule 402; Relevant Evidence Generally Admissible; Irrelevant Evidence Inadmissible

All relevant evidence is admissible, except as otherwise provided by the Constitution of the United States, the Constitution of the State of Michigan, these rules, or other rules adopted by the Supreme Court. Evidence which is not relevant is not admissible.

Rule 403; Exclusion of Relevant Evidence on Grounds of Prejudice, Confusion, or Waste of Time

Although relevant, evidence may be excluded if its probative value is substantially outweighed by the danger of unfair prejudice, confusion of the issues, or misleading the jury, or by considerations of undue delay, waste of time, or needless presentation of cumulative evidence.

Rule 404; Character Evidence Not Admissible to Prove Conduct; Exceptions; Other Crimes

(a) **Character evidence generally.** Evidence of a person's character or a trait of character is not admissible for the purpose of proving action in conformity therewith on a particular occasion, except:

(1) *Character of accused.* Evidence of a pertinent trait of character offered by an accused, or by the prosecution to rebut the same; or if evidence of a trait of character of the alleged victim of the crime is offered by the accused and admitted under subdivision (a)(2), evidence of a trait of character for aggression of the accused offered by the prosecution;

(2) *Character of alleged victim of homicide.* When self-defense is an issue in a charge of homicide, evidence of a trait of character for aggression of the alleged victim of the crime offered by an accused, or evidence offered by the prosecution to rebut the same, or evidence of a character trait of peacefulness of the alleged victim offered by the prosecution in a charge of homicide to rebut evidence that the alleged victim was the first aggressor;

(3) *Character of alleged victim of sexual conduct crime.* In a prosecution for criminal sexual conduct, evidence of the alleged victim's past sexual conduct with the defendant and evidence of specific instances of sexual activity showing the source or origin of semen, pregnancy, or disease;

(4) *Character of witness.* Evidence of the character of a witness, as provided in Rules 607, 608, and 609.

(b) **Other crimes, wrongs, or acts.**

(1) Evidence of other crimes, wrongs, or acts is not admissible to prove the character of a person in order to show action in conformity therewith. It may, however, be admissible for other purposes, such as proof of motive, opportunity, intent, preparation,

scheme, plan, or system in doing an act, knowledge, identity, or absence of mistake or accident when the same is material, whether such other crimes, wrongs, or acts are contemporaneous with, or prior or subsequent to the conduct at issue in the case.

(2) The prosecution in a criminal case shall provide reasonable notice in advance of trial, or during trial if the court excuses pretrial notice on good cause shown, of the general nature of any such evidence it intends to introduce at trial and the rationale, whether or not mentioned in subparagraph (b)(1), for admitting the evidence. If necessary to a determination of the admissibility of the evidence under this rule, the defendant shall be required to state the theory or theories of defense, limited only by the defendant's privilege against self-incrimination.

Rule 405; Methods of Proving Character

(a) **Reputation or opinion**. In all cases in which evidence of character or a trait of character of a person is admissible, proof may be made by testimony as to reputation or by testimony in the form of an opinion. On cross-examination, inquiry is allowable into reports of relevant specific instances of conduct.

(b) **Specific instances of conduct**. In cases in which character or a trait of character of a person is an essential element of a charge, claim, or defense, proof may also be made of specific instances of that person's conduct.

Rule 406 Habit; Routine Practice

Evidence of the habit of a person or of the routine practice of an organization, whether corroborated or not and regardless of the presence of eyewitnesses, is relevant to prove that the conduct of the person or organization on a particular occasion was in conformity with the habit or routine practice.

Rule 407; Subsequent Remedial Measures

When, after an event, measures are taken which, if taken previously, would have made the event less likely to occur, evidence of the subsequent measures is not admissible to prove negligence or culpable conduct in connection with the event. This rule does not require the exclusion of evidence of subsequent measures when offered for another purpose, such as proving ownership, control, or feasibility of precautionary measures, if controverted, or impeachment.

Rule 408; Compromise and Offers to Compromise

Evidence of (1) furnishing or offering or promising to furnish, or (2) accepting or offering or promising to accept, a valuable consideration in compromising or attempting to compromise a claim which was disputed as to either validity or amount, is not admissible to prove liability for or invalidity of the claim or its amount. Evidence of conduct or statements made in compromise negotiations is likewise not admissible. This rule does not require the exclusion of any evidence otherwise discoverable merely because it is presented in the course of compromise negotiations. This rule also does not require exclusion when the evidence is offered for another purpose, such as proving bias or prejudice of a witness, negativing a contention of undue delay, or proving an effort to obstruct a criminal investigation or prosecution.

Rule 409; Payment of Medical and Similar Expenses

Evidence of furnishing or offering or promising to pay medical, hospital, or similar expenses occasioned by an injury is not admissible to prove liability for the injury.

Rule 410; Inadmissibility of Pleas, Plea Discussions, and Related Statements

Except as otherwise provided in this rule, evidence of the following is not, in any civil or criminal proceeding, admissible against the defendant who made the plea or was a participant in the plea discussions:

(1) A plea of guilty which was later withdrawn;

(2) A plea of nolo contendere, except that, to the extent that evidence of a guilty plea would be admissible, evidence of a plea of nolo contendere to a criminal charge may be admitted in a civil proceeding to support a defense against a claim asserted by the person who entered the plea;

(3) Any statement made in the course of any proceedings under MCR 6.302 or comparable state or federal procedure regarding either of the foregoing pleas; or

(4) Any statement made in the course of plea discussions with an attorney for the prosecuting authority which do not result in a plea of guilty or which result in a plea of guilty later withdrawn.

However, such a statement is admissible (i) in any proceeding wherein another statement made in the course of the same plea or plea discussions has been introduced and the statement ought in fairness be considered contemporaneously with it, or (ii) in a criminal proceeding for perjury or false statement if the statement was made by the defendant under oath, on the record and in the presence of counsel.

Rule 411; Liability Insurance

Evidence that a person was or was not insured against liability is not admissible upon the issue whether the person acted negligently or otherwise wrongfully. This rule does not require the exclusion of evidence of insurance against liability when offered for another purpose, such as proof of agency, ownership, or control, if controverted, or bias or prejudice of a witness.

Part V – Privileges

Rule 501; Privilege; General Rule

Privilege is governed by the common law, except as modified by statute or court rule.

Part VI – Witnesses

Rule 601; Witnesses; General Rule of Competency

Unless the court finds after questioning a person that the person does not have sufficient physical or mental capacity or sense of obligation to testify truthfully and understandably, every person is competent to be a witness except as otherwise provided in these rules.

Rule 602; Lack of Personal Knowledge

A witness may not testify to a matter unless evidence is introduced sufficient to support a finding that the witness has personal knowledge of the matter. Evidence to prove personal knowledge may, but need not, consist of the witness' own testimony. This rule is subject to the provisions of Rule 703, relating to opinion testimony by expert witnesses.

Rule 603; Oath or Affirmation

Before testifying, every witness shall be required to declare that the witness will testify truthfully, by oath or affirmation administered in a form calculated to awaken the witness' conscience and impress the witness' mind with the duty to do so.

Rule 604; Interpreters

An interpreter is subject to the provisions of these rules relating to qualification as an expert and the administration of an oath or affirmation to make a true translation.

Rule 605; Competency of Judge as Witness

The judge presiding at the trial may not testify in that trial as a witness. No objection need be made in order to preserve the point.

Rule 606; Competency of Juror as Witness

(a) **At the trial**. A member of the jury may not testify as a witness before that jury in the trial of the case in which the juror is sitting. No objection need be made in order to preserve the point.

(b) **Inquiry into validity of verdict or indictment**. Upon an inquiry into the validity of a verdict or indictment, a juror may not testify as to any matter or statement occurring during the course of the jury's deliberations or to the effect of anything upon that or any other juror's mind or emotions as influencing the juror to assent to or dissent from the verdict or indictment or concerning the juror's mental processes in connection therewith. But a juror may testify about (1) whether extraneous prejudicial information was improperly brought to the jury's attention, (2) whether any outside influence was improperly brought to bear upon any juror, or (3) whether there was a mistake in entering the verdict onto the verdict form. A juror's affidavit or evidence of any statement by the juror may not be received on a matter about which the juror would be precluded from testifying.

Rule 607; Who May Impeach

The credibility of a witness may be attacked by any party, including the party calling the witness.

Rule 608; Evidence of Character and Conduct of Witness

(a) **Opinion and reputation evidence of character.** The credibility of a witness may be attacked or supported by evidence in the form of opinion or reputation, but subject to these limitations: (1) the evidence may refer only to character for truthfulness or untruthfulness, and (2) evidence of truthful character is admissible only after the character of the witness for truthfulness has been attacked by opinion or reputation evidence or otherwise.

(b) **Specific instances of conduct.** Specific instances of the conduct of a witness, for the purpose of attacking or supporting the witness' credibility, other than conviction of crime as provided in Rule 609, may not be proved by extrinsic evidence. They may, however, in the discretion of the court, if probative of truthfulness or untruthfulness, be inquired into on cross-examination of the witness (1) concerning the witness' character for truthfulness or untruthfulness, or (2) concerning the character for truthfulness or untruthfulness of another witness as to which character the witness being cross-examined has testified. The giving of testimony, whether by an accused or by any other witness, does not operate as a waiver of the accused's or the witness' privilege against self-incrimination when examined with respect to matters which relate only to credibility.

Rule 609; Impeachment by Evidence of Conviction of Crime

(a) **General rule.** For the purpose of attacking the credibility of a witness, evidence that the witness has been convicted of a crime shall not be admitted unless the evidence has been elicited from the witness or established by public record during cross-examination, and

(1) the crime contained an element of dishonesty or false statement, or

(2) the crime contained an element of theft, and

   (A) the crime was punishable by imprisonment in excess of one year or death under the law under which the witness was convicted, and

   (B) the court determines that the evidence has significant probative value on the issue of credibility and, if the witness is the defendant in a criminal trial, the court further determines that the probative value of the evidence outweighs its prejudicial effect.

(b) **Determining probative value and prejudicial effect**. For purposes of the probative value determination required by subrule (a)(2)(B), the court shall consider only the age of the conviction and the degree to which a conviction of the crime is indicative of veracity. If a determination of prejudicial effect is required, the court shall consider only the conviction's similarity to the charged offense and the possible effects on the decisional process if admitting the evidence causes the defendant to elect not to testify. The court must articulate, on the record, the analysis of each factor.

(c) **Time limit**. Evidence of a conviction under this rule is not admissible if a period of more than ten years has elapsed since the date of the conviction or of the release of the witness from the confinement imposed for that conviction, whichever is the later date.

(d) **Effect of pardon, annulment, or certificate of rehabilitation.** Evidence of a conviction is not admissible under this rule if (1) the conviction has been the subject of a pardon, annulment, certificate of rehabilitation, or other equivalent procedure based on a finding of the rehabilitation of the person convicted, and that person has not been convicted of a subsequent crime which was punishable by death or imprisonment in excess of one year, or (2) the conviction has been the subject of a pardon, annulment, or other equivalent procedure based on a finding of innocence.

(e) **Juvenile adjudications.** Evidence of juvenile adjudications is generally not admissible under this rule, except in subsequent cases against the same child in the juvenile division of a probate court. The court may, however, in a criminal case or a juvenile proceeding against the child allow evidence of a juvenile adjudication of a witness other than the accused if conviction of the offense would be admissible to attack the credibility of an adult and the court is satisfied that admission is necessary for a fair determination of the case or proceeding.

(f) **Pendency of appeal.** The pendency of an appeal therefrom does not render evidence of a conviction inadmissible. Evidence of the pendency of an appeal is admissible.

Rule 610; Religious Beliefs or Opinions

Evidence of the beliefs or opinions of a witness on matters of religion is not admissible for the purpose of showing that by reason of their nature the witness' credibility is impaired or enhanced.

Rule 611; Mode and Order of Interrogation and Presentation

(a) **Control by court.** The court shall exercise reasonable control over the mode and order of interrogating witnesses and presenting evidence so as to (1) make the interrogation and presentation effective for the ascertainment of the truth, (2) avoid needless consumption of time, and (3) protect witnesses from harassment or undue embarrassment.

(b) **Appearance of Parties and Witnesses.** The court shall exercise reasonable control over the appearance of parties and witnesses so as to (1) ensure that the demeanor of such persons may be observed and assessed by the fact-finder and (2) ensure the accurate identification of such persons.

(c) **Scope of cross-examination.** A witness may be cross-examined on any matter relevant to any issue in the case, including credibility. The judge may limit cross-examination with respect to matters not testified to on direct examination.

(d) **Leading Questions.**

(1) Leading questions should not be used on the direct examination of a witness except as may be necessary to develop the witness' testimony.

(2) Ordinarily leading questions should be permitted on cross-examination. (3) When a party calls a hostile witness, an adverse party or a witness identified with an adverse party, interrogation may be by leading questions. It is not necessary to declare the intent to ask leading questions before the questioning begins or before the questioning moves beyond preliminary inquiries.

Rule 612; Writing or Object Used to Refresh Memory

(a) **While testifying.** If, while testifying, a witness uses a writing or object to refresh memory, an adverse party is entitled to have the writing or object produced at the trial, hearing, or deposition in which the witness is testifying.

(b) **Before testifying.** If, before testifying, a witness uses a writing or object to refresh memory for the purpose of testifying and the court in its discretion determines that the interests of justice so require, an adverse party is entitled to have the writing or object produced, if practicable, at the trial, hearing, or deposition in which the witness is testifying.

(c) **Terms and conditions of production and use.** A party entitled to have a writing or object produced under this rule is entitled to inspect it, to cross-examine the witness thereon, and to introduce in evidence, for their bearing on credibility only unless otherwise admissible under these rules for another purpose, those portions which relate to the testimony of the witness. If production of the writing or object at the trial, hearing, or deposition is impracticable, the court may order it made available for inspection. If it is claimed that the writing or object contains matters not related to the subject matter of the testimony the court shall examine the writing or object in camera, excise any portions not so related, and order delivery of the remainder to the party entitled thereto. Any portion withheld over objections shall be preserved and made available to the appellate court in the event of an appeal. If a writing or object is not produced, made available for inspection, or delivered pursuant to order under this rule, the court shall make any order justice requires, except that in criminal cases when the prosecution elects not to comply, the order shall be one striking the testimony or, if the court in its discretion determines that the interests of justice so require, declaring a mistrial.

Rule 613; Prior Statements of Witnesses

(a) **Examining witness concerning prior statement.** In examining a witness concerning a prior statement made by the witness, whether written or not, the statement need not be shown nor its contents disclosed to the witness at that time, but on request it shall be shown or disclosed to opposing counsel and the witness.

(b) **Extrinsic evidence of prior inconsistent statement of witness.** Extrinsic evidence of a prior inconsistent statement by a witness is not admissible unless the witness is afforded an opportunity to explain or deny the same and the opposite party is afforded an opportunity to interrogate the witness thereon, or the interests of justice otherwise require. This provision does not apply to admissions of a party- opponent as defined in Rule 801(d)(2).

Rule 614; Calling and Interrogation of Witnesses by Court

(a) **Calling by court.** The court may, on its own motion or at the suggestion of a party, call witnesses, and all parties are entitled to cross-examine witnesses thus called.

(b) **Interrogation by court.** The court may interrogate witnesses, whether called by itself or by a party.

(c) **Objections.** Objections to the calling of witnesses by the court or to interrogation by it may be made at the time or at the next available opportunity when the jury is not present.

Rule 615; Exclusion of Witnesses

At the request of a party the court may order witnesses excluded so that they cannot hear the testimony of other witnesses, and it may make the order of its own motion. This rule does not authorize exclusion of (1) a party who is a natural person, or (2) an officer or employee of a party which is not a natural person designated as its representative by its attorney, or (3) a person whose presence is shown by a party to be essential to the presentation of the party's cause.

PART VII – Opinion and Expert Testimony

Rule 701; Opinion Testimony by Lay Witnesses

If the witness is not testifying as an expert, the witness' testimony in the form of opinions or inferences is limited to those opinions or inferences which are (a) rationally based on the perception of the witness and (b) helpful to a clear understanding of the witness' testimony or the determination of a fact in issue.

Rule 702; Testimony by Experts

If the court determines that scientific, technical, or other specialized knowledge will assist the trier of fact to understand the evidence or to determine a fact in issue, a witness qualified as an expert by knowledge, skill, experience, training, or education may testify thereto in the form of an opinion or otherwise if (1) the testimony is based on sufficient facts or data, (2) the testimony is the product of reliable principles and methods, and (3) the witness has applied the principles and methods reliably to the facts of the case.

Rule 703; Bases of Opinion Testimony by Experts

The facts or data in the particular case upon which an expert bases an opinion or inference shall be in evidence. This rule does not restrict the discretion of the court to receive expert opinion testimony subject to the condition that the factual bases of the opinion be admitted in evidence hereafter.

Rule 704; Opinion on Ultimate Issue

Testimony in the form of an opinion or inference otherwise admissible is not objectionable because it embraces an ultimate issue to be decided by the trier of fact.

Rule 705; Disclosure of Facts or Data Underlying Expert Opinion

The expert may testify in terms of opinion or inference and give reasons therefor without prior disclosure of the underlying facts or data, unless the court requires otherwise. The expert may in any event be required to disclose the underlying facts or data on cross-examination.

Rule 706; Court-Appointed Experts

(a) **Appointment**. The court may on its own motion or on the motion of any party enter an order to show cause why expert witnesses should not be appointed, and may request the parties to submit nominations. The court may appoint any expert witnesses agreed upon by the parties, and may appoint expert witnesses of its own selection. An expert witness shall not be appointed by the court unless the witness consents to act. A witness so appointed shall be informed of the witness' duties by the court in writing, a copy of which shall be filed with the clerk, or at a conference in which the parties shall have opportunity to participate. A witness so appointed shall advise the parties of the witness' findings, if any; the witness' deposition may be taken by any party; and the witness may be called to testify by the court or any party. The witness shall be subject to cross-examination by each party, including a party calling the witness.

(b) **Compensation**. Expert witnesses so appointed are entitled to reasonable compensation in whatever sum the court may allow. The compensation thus fixed is payable from funds which may be provided by law in criminal cases and civil actions and proceedings involving just compensation under the Fifth Amendment. In other civil actions and proceedings the compensation shall be paid by the parties in such proportion and at such time as the court directs, and thereafter charged in like manner as other costs.

(c) **Disclosure of appointment**. In the exercise of its discretion, the court may authorize disclosure to the jury of the fact that the court appointed the expert witness.

(d) **Parties' experts of own selection**. Nothing in this rule limits the parties in calling expert witnesses of their own selection. Rule 707 Use of Learned Treatises for Impeachment

To the extent called to the attention of an expert witness upon cross-examination, statements contained in published treatises, periodicals, or pamphlets on a subject of history, medicine, or other science or art, established as a reliable authority by the testimony or admission of the witness or by other expert testimony or by judicial notice, are admissible for impeachment purposes only. If admitted, the statements may be read into evidence but may not be received as exhibits.

Part VIII – Hearsay

Rule 801; Hearsay; Definitions

The following definitions apply under this article:

(a) **Statement**. A "statement" is (1) an oral or written assertion or (2) nonverbal conduct of a person, if it is intended by the person as an assertion.

(b) **Declarant**. A "declarant" is a person who makes a statement.

(c) **Hearsay**. "Hearsay" is a statement, other than the one made by the declarant while testifying at the trial or hearing, offered in evidence to prove the truth of the matter asserted.

(d) **Statements which are not hearsay.** A statement is not hearsay if–

   (1) *Prior statement of witness*. The declarant testifies at the trial or hearing and is subject to cross-examination concerning the statement, and the statement is (A) inconsistent with the declarant's testimony, and was given under oath subject to the penalty of perjury at a trial, hearing, or other proceeding, or in a deposition, or (B) consistent with the declarant's testimony and is offered to rebut an express or implied charge against the declarant of recent fabrication or improper influence or motive, or (C) one of identification of a person made after perceiving the person; or

(2) *Admission by party-opponent.* The statement is offered against a party and is (A) the party's own statement, in either an individual or a representative capacity, except statements made in connection with a guilty plea to a misdemeanor motor vehicle violation or an admission of responsibility for a civil infraction under laws pertaining to motor vehicles, or (B) a statement of which the party has manifested an adoption or belief in its truth, or (C) a statement by a person authorized by the party to make a statement concerning the subject, or (D) a statement by the party's agent or servant concerning a matter within the scope of the agency or employment, made during the existence of the relationship, or (E) a statement by a coconspirator of a party during the course and in furtherance of the conspiracy on independent proof of the conspiracy.

Rule 802; Hearsay Rule

Hearsay is not admissible except as provided by these rules.

Rule 803; Hearsay Exceptions; Availability of Declarant Immaterial

The following are not excluded by the hearsay rule, even though the declarant is available as a witness:

(1) *Present sense impression.* A statement describing or explaining an event or condition made while the declarant was perceiving the event or condition, or immediately thereafter.

(2) *Excited utterance.* A statement relating to a startling event or condition made while the declarant was under

the stress of excitement caused by the event or condition.

(3) *Then existing mental, emotional, or physical condition.* A statement of the declarant's then existing state of mind, emotion, sensation, or physical condition (such as intent, plan, motive, design, mental feeling, pain, and bodily health), but not including a statement of memory or belief to prove the fact remembered or believed unless it relates to the execution, revocation, identification, or terms of declarant's will.

(4) *Statements made for purposes of medical treatment or medical diagnosis in connection with treatment.* Statements made for purposes of medical treatment or medical diagnosis in connection with treatment and describing medical history, or past or present symptoms, pain, or sensations, or the inception or general character of the cause or external source thereof insofar as reasonably necessary to such diagnosis and treatment.

(5) *Recorded recollection.* A memorandum or record concerning a matter about which a witness once had knowledge but now has insufficient recollection to enable the witness to testify fully and accurately, shown to have been made or adopted by the witness when the matter was fresh in the witness' memory and to reflect that knowledge correctly. If admitted, the memorandum or record may be read into evidence but may not itself be received as an exhibit unless offered by an adverse party.

(6) *Records of regularly conducted activity.* A memorandum, report, record, or data compilation, in

any form, of acts, transactions, occurrences, events, conditions, opinions, or diagnoses, made at or near the time by, or from information transmitted by, a person with knowledge, if kept in the course of a regularly conducted business activity, and if it was the regular practice of that business activity to make the memorandum, report, record, or data compilation, all as shown by the testimony of the custodian or other qualified witness, or by certification that complies with a rule promulgated by the supreme court or a statute permitting certification, unless the source of information or the method or circumstances of preparation indicate lack of trustworthiness. The term "business" as used in this paragraph includes business, institution, association, profession, occupation, and calling of every kind, whether or not conducted for profit.

(7) *Absence of entry in records kept in accordance with the provisions of paragraph (6).* Evidence that a matter is not included in the memoranda, reports, records, or data compilations, in any form, kept in accordance with the provisions of paragraph (6), to prove the nonoccurrence or nonexistence of the matter, if the matter was of a kind of which a memorandum, report, record, or data compilation was regularly made and preserved, unless the sources of information or other circumstances indicate lack of trustworthiness.

(8) *Public records and reports.* Records, reports, statements, or data compilations, in any form, of public offices or agencies, setting forth (A) the activities of the office or agency, or (B) matters observed pursuant to duty imposed by law as to which matters there was a duty to report, excluding, however, in criminal cases

matters observed by police officers and other law enforcement personnel, and subject to the limitations of MCL 257.624.

(9) *Records of vital statistics.* Records or data compilations, in any form, of births, fetal deaths, deaths, or marriages, if the report thereof was made to a public office pursuant to requirements of law.

(10) *Absence of public record or entry.* To prove the absence of a record, report, statement, or data compilation, in any form, or the nonoccurrence or nonexistence of a matter of which a record, report, statement, or data compilation, in any form, was regularly made and preserved by a public office or agency, evidence in the form of a certification in accordance with Rule 902, or testimony, that diligent search failed to disclose the record, report, statement, or data compilation, or entry.

(11) *Records of religious organizations.* Statements of births, marriages, divorces, deaths, legitimacy, ancestry, relationship by blood or marriage, or other similar facts of personal or family history, contained in a regularly kept record of a religious organization.

(12) *Marriage, baptismal, and similar certificates.* Statements of fact contained in a certificate that the maker performed a marriage or other ceremony or administered a sacrament, made by a member of the clergy, public official, or other person authorized by the rules or practices of a religious organization or by law to perform the act certified, and purporting to have been issued at the time of the act or within a reasonable time thereafter.

(13) *Family records.* Statements of fact concerning personal or family history contained in family Bibles, genealogies, charts, engravings on rings, inscriptions on family portraits, engravings on urns, crypts, or tombstones, or the like.

(14) *Records of documents affecting an interest in property.* The record of a document purporting to establish or affect an interest in property, as proof of the content of the original recorded document and its execution and delivery by each person by whom it purports to have been executed, if the record is a record of a public office and an applicable statute authorizes the recording of documents of that kind in that office.

(15) *Statements in documents affecting an interest in property.* A statement contained in a document purporting to establish or affect an interest in property if the matter stated was relevant to the purpose of the document, unless dealings with the property since the document was made have been inconsistent with the truth of the statement or the purport of the document.

(16) *Statements in ancient documents.* Statements in a document in existence twenty years or more the authenticity of which is established.

(17) *Market reports, commercial publications.* Market quotations, tabulations, lists, directories, or other published compilations, generally used and relied upon by the public or by persons in particular occupations.

(18) *Deposition testimony of an expert.* Testimony given as a witness in a deposition taken in compliance with law in the course of the same proceeding if the court finds that

the deponent is an expert witness and if the deponent is not a party to the proceeding.

(19) *Reputation concerning personal or family history.* Reputation among members of a person's family by blood, adoption, or marriage, or among a person's associates, or in the community, concerning a person's birth, adoption, marriage, divorce, death, legitimacy, relationship by blood, adoption, or marriage, ancestry, or other similar fact of personal or family history.

(20) *Reputation concerning boundaries or general history.* Reputation in a community, arising before the controversy, as to boundaries of or customs affecting lands in the community, and reputation as to events of general history important to the community or state or nation in which located.

(21) *Reputation as to character.* Reputation of a person's character among associates or in the community.

(22) *Judgment of previous conviction.* Evidence of a final judgment, entered after a trial or upon a plea of guilty (or upon a plea of nolo contendere if evidence of the plea is not excluded by MRE 410), adjudging a person guilty of a crime punishable by death or imprisonment in excess of one year, to prove any fact essential to sustain the judgment, but not including, when offered by the state in a criminal prosecution for purposes other than impeachment, judgments against persons other than the accused. The pendency of an appeal may be shown but does not affect admissibility.

(23) *Judgment as to personal, family, or general history, or boundaries.* Judgments as proof of matters of personal,

family or general history, or boundaries, essential to the judgment, if the same would be provable by evidence of reputation.

(24) *Other Exceptions.* A statement not specifically covered by any of the foregoing exceptions but having equivalent circumstantial guarantees of trustworthiness, if the court determines that (A) the statement is offered as evidence of a material fact, (B) the statement is more probative on the point for which it is offered than any other evidence that the proponent can procure through reasonable efforts, and (C) the general purposes of these rules and the interests of justice will best be served by admission of the statement into evidence. However, a statement may not be admitted under this exception unless the proponent of the statement makes known to the adverse party, sufficiently in advance of the trial or hearing to provide the adverse party with a fair opportunity to prepare to meet it, the proponent's intention to offer the statement and the particulars of it, including the name and address of the declarant.

Rule 803A; Hearsay Exception; Child's Statement About Sexual Act

A statement describing an incident that included a sexual act performed with or on the declarant by the defendant or an accomplice is admissible to the extent that it corroborates testimony given by the declarant during the same proceeding, provided:

(1) the declarant was under the age of ten when the statement was made;

(2) the statement is shown to have been spontaneous and without indication of manufacture;

(3) either the declarant made the statement immediately after the incident or any delay is excusable as having been caused by fear or other equally effective circumstance; and

(4) the statement is introduced through the testimony of someone other than the declarant.

If the declarant made more than one corroborative statement about the incident, only the first is admissible under this rule.

A statement may not be admitted under this rule unless the proponent of the statement makes known to the adverse party the intent to offer the statement, and the particulars of the statement, sufficiently in advance of the trial or hearing to provide the adverse party with a fair opportunity to prepare to meet the statement.

This rule applies in criminal and delinquency proceedings only.

Rule 804; Hearsay Exceptions; Declarant Unavailable

(a) **Definition of unavailability.** "Unavailability as a witness" includes situations in which the declarant–

(1) is exempted by ruling of the court on the ground of privilege from testifying concerning the subject matter of the declarant's statement; or

(2) persists in refusing to testify concerning the subject matter of the declarant's statement despite an order of the court to do so; or

(3) has a lack of memory of the subject matter of the declarant's statement; or

(4) is unable to be present or to testify at the hearing because of death or then existing physical or mental illness or infirmity; or

(5) is absent from the hearing and the proponent of a statement has been unable to procure the declarant's attendance (or in the case of a hearsay exception under subdivision (b)(2), (3), or (4), the declarant's attendance or testimony) by process or other reasonable means, and in a criminal case, due diligence is shown.

A declarant is not unavailable as a witness if exemption, refusal, claim of lack of memory, inability, or absence is due to the procurement or wrongdoing of the proponent of a statement for the purpose of preventing the witness from attending or testifying.

(b) **Hearsay exceptions.** The following are not excluded by the hearsay rule if the declarant is unavailable as a witness:

(1) *Former testimony.* Testimony given as a witness at another hearing of the same or a different proceeding, if the party against whom the testimony is now offered, or, in a civil action or proceeding, a predecessor in interest, had an opportunity and

similar motive to develop the testimony by direct, cross, or redirect examination.

(2) *Statement under belief of impending death.* In a prosecution for homicide or in a civil action or proceeding, a statement made by a declarant while believing that the declarant's death was imminent, concerning the cause or circumstances of what the declarant believed to be impending death.

(3) *Statement against interest.* A statement which was at the time of its making so far contrary to the declarant's pecuniary or proprietary interest, or so far tended to subject the declarant to civil or criminal liability, or to render invalid a claim by the declarant against another, that a reasonable person in the declarant's position would not have made the statement unless believing it to be true. A statement tending to expose the declarant to criminal liability and offered to exculpate the accused is not admissible unless corroborating circumstances clearly indicate the trustworthiness of the statement.

(4) *Statement of personal or family history.* (A) A statement concerning the declarant's own birth, adoption, marriage, divorce, legitimacy, relationship by blood, adoption, or marriage, ancestry, or other similar fact of personal or family history, even though declarant had no means of acquiring personal knowledge of the matter stated; or (B) a statement concerning the foregoing matters, and death also, of another person, if the declarant was related to the other by blood, adoption, or marriage or was so intimately associated with the other's family as to be

likely to have accurate information concerning the matter declared.

(5) *Deposition Testimony*. Testimony given as a witness in a deposition taken in compliance with law in the course of the same or another proceeding, if the party against whom the testimony is now offered, or, in a civil action or proceeding, a predecessor in interest, had an opportunity and similar motive to develop the testimony by direct, cross, or redirect examination.

For purposes of this subsection only, "unavailability of a witness" also includes situations in which:

(A) The witness is at a greater distance than 100 miles from the place of trial or hearing, or is out of the United States, unless it appears that the absence of the witness was procured by the party offering the deposition; or

(B) On motion and notice, such exceptional circumstances exist as to make it desirable, in the interests of justice, and with due regard to the importance of presenting the testimony of witnesses orally in open court, to allow the deposition to be used.

(6) *Statement by declarant made unavailable by opponent*. A statement offered against a party that has engaged in or encouraged wrongdoing that was intended to, and did, procure the unavailability of the declarant as a witness.

(7) *Other Exceptions*. A statement not specifically covered by any of the foregoing exceptions but

having equivalent circumstantial guarantees of trustworthiness, if the court determines that (A) the statement is offered as evidence of a material fact, (B) the statement is more probative on the point for which it is offered than any other evidence that the proponent can procure through reasonable efforts, and (C) the general purposes of these rules and the interests of justice will best be served by admission of the statement into evidence. However, a statement may not be admitted under this exception unless the proponent of the statement makes known to the adverse party, sufficiently in advance of the trial or hearing to provide the adverse party with a fair opportunity to prepare to meet it, the proponent's intention to offer the statement and the particulars of it, including the name and address of the declarant.

Rule 805; Hearsay Within Hearsay

Hearsay included within hearsay is not excluded under the hearsay rule if each part of the combined statements conforms with an exception to the hearsay rule provided in these rules.

Rule 806; Attacking and Supporting Credibility of Declarant

When a hearsay statement, or a statement defined in Rule 801(d)(2)(C), (D), or (E), has been admitted in evidence, the credibility of the declarant may be attacked, and if attacked may be supported, by any evidence which would be admissible for those purposes if declarant had testified as a witness. Evidence of a statement or conduct by the declarant at any time, inconsistent with the declarant's hearsay statement, is not subject to any requirement that the declarant may have been afforded an opportunity to deny or explain. If the party against whom a hearsay statement has been admitted calls the declarant as a witness, the party is entitled to examine the declarant on the statement as if under cross-examination.

PART IX – Authentication and Identification

Rule 901; Requirement of Authentication or Identification

(a) **General provision.** The requirement of authentication or identification as a condition precedent to admissibility is satisfied by evidence sufficient to support a finding that the matter in question is what its proponent claims.

(b) **Illustrations.** By way of illustration only, and not by way of limitation, the following are examples of authentication or identification conforming with the requirements of this rule:

   (1) *Testimony of witness with knowledge.* Testimony that a matter is what it is claimed to be.

   (2) *Nonexpert opinion on handwriting.* Nonexpert opinion as to the genuineness of handwriting, based upon familiarity not acquired for purposes of the litigation.

   (3) *Comparison by trier or expert witness.* Comparison by the trier of fact or by expert witnesses with specimens which have been authenticated.

   (4) *Distinctive characteristics and the like.* Appearance, contents, substance, internal patterns, or other distinctive characteristics, taken in conjunction with circumstances.

   (5) *Voice identification.* Identification of a voice, whether heard firsthand or through mechanical or electronic transmission or recording, by opinion

based upon hearing the voice at any time under circumstances connecting it with the alleged speaker.

(6) *Telephone conversations.* Telephone conversations, by evidence that a call was made to the number assigned at the time by the telephone company to a particular person or business, if (A) in the case of a person, circumstances, including self-identification, show the person answering to be the one called, or (B) in the case of a business, the call was made to a place of business and the conversation related to business reasonably transacted over the telephone.

(7) *Public records or reports.* Evidence that a writing authorized by law to be recorded or filed and in fact recorded or filed in a public office, or a purported public record, report, statement, or data compilation, in any form, is from the public office where items of this nature are kept.

(8) *Ancient documents or data compilation.* Evidence that a document or data compilation, in any form, (A) is in such condition as to create no suspicion concerning its authenticity, (B) was in a place where it, if authentic, would likely be, and (C) has been in existence 20 years or more at the time it is offered.

(9) *Process or system.* Evidence describing a process or system used to produce a result and showing that the process or system produces an accurate result.

(10) *Methods provided by statute or rule.* Any method of authentication or identification provided by the

Supreme Court of Michigan or by a Michigan statute.

Rule 902; Self-Authentication

Extrinsic evidence of authenticity as a condition precedent to admissibility is not required with respect to the following:

(1) *Domestic public documents under seal.* A document bearing a seal purporting to be that of the United States, or of any state, district, commonwealth, territory, or insular possession thereof, or the Panama Canal Zone, or the Trust Territory of the Pacific Islands, or of a political subdivision, department, officer, or agency thereof, and a signature purporting to be an attestation or execution.

(2) *Domestic public documents not under seal.* A document purporting to bear the signature in the official capacity of an officer or employee of any entity included in paragraph (1) hereof, having no seal, if a public officer having a seal and having official duties in the district or political subdivision of the officer or employee certifies under seal that the signer has the official capacity and that the signature is genuine.

(3) *Foreign public documents.* A document purporting to be executed or attested in an official capacity by a person authorized by the laws of a foreign country to make the execution or attestation, and accompanied by a final certification as to the genuineness of the signature and official position (A) of the executing or attesting person, or (B) of any foreign official whose certificate of genuineness of signature and official position relates to the execution or attestation or is in a chain of certificates of genuineness of signature and official position relating

to the execution or attestation. A final certification may be made by a secretary of embassy or legation, consul general, consul, vice consul, or consular agent of the United States, or a diplomatic or consular official of the foreign country assigned or accredited to the United States. If reasonable opportunity has been given to all parties to investigate the authenticity and accuracy of official documents, the court may, for good cause shown, order that they be treated as presumptively authentic without final certification or permit them to be evidenced by an attested summary with or without final certification.

(4) *Certified copies of public records.* A copy of an official record or report or entry therein, or of a document authorized by law to be recorded or filed and actually recorded or filed in a public office, including data compilations in any form, certified as correct by the custodian or other person authorized to make the certification, by certificate complying with paragraph (1), (2), or (3) or complying with any law of the United States or of this state.

(5) *Official publications.* Books, pamphlets, or other publications purporting to be issued by public authority.

(6) *Newspapers and periodicals.* Printed materials purporting to be newspapers or periodicals.

(7) *Trade inscriptions and the like.* Inscriptions, signs, tags, or labels purporting to have been affixed in the course of business and indicating ownership, control, or origin.

(8) *Acknowledged documents.* Documents accompanied by a certificate of acknowledgment executed in the manner

provided by law by a notary public or other officer authorized by law to take acknowledgments.

(9) *Commercial paper and related documents.* Commercial paper, signatures thereon, and documents relating thereto to the extent provided by general commercial law.

(10) *Presumptions created by law.* Any signature, document, or other matter declared by any law of the United States or of this state to be presumptively or prima facie genuine or authentic.

(11) *Certified records of regularly conducted activity.* The original or a duplicate of a record, whether domestic or foreign, of regularly conducted business activity that would be admissible under rule 803(6), if accompanied by a written declaration under oath by its custodian or other qualified person certifying that

> (A) The record was made at or near the time of the occurrence of the matters set forth by, or from information transmitted by, a person with knowledge of those matters;
>
> (B) The record was kept in the course of the regularly conducted business activity; and
>
> (C) It was the regular practice of the business activity to make the record.

A party intending to offer a record into evidence under this paragraph must provide written notice of that intention to all adverse parties, and must make the record and declaration available for inspection sufficiently in advance of their offer into evidence to provide an adverse party with a fair opportunity to challenge them.

Rule 903; Subscribing Witness' Testimony Unnecessary

The testimony of a subscribing witness is not necessary to authenticate a writing unless required by the laws of the jurisdiction whose laws govern the validity of the writing.

PART X – Contents of Writings, Recordings, and Photographs

Rule 1001; Contents of Writings, Recordings, and Photographs; Definitions

For purposes of this article the following definitions are applicable:

(1) *Writings and recordings.* "Writings" and "recordings" consist of letters, words, or numbers, or their equivalent, set down by handwriting, typewriting, printing, photostating, photographing, magnetic impulse, mechanical or electronic recording, or other form of data compilation.

(2) *Photographs.* "Photographs" include still photographs, x-ray films, video tapes, and motion pictures.

(3) *Original.* An "original" of a writing or recording is the writing or recording itself or any counterpart intended to have the same effect by a person executing or issuing it. An "original" of a photograph includes the negative or any print therefrom. If data are stored in a computer or similar device, any printout or other output readable by sight, shown to reflect the data accurately, is an "original."

(4) *Duplicate.* A "duplicate" is a counterpart produced by the same impression as the original, or from the same matrix, or by means of photography, including enlargements and miniatures, or by mechanical or electronic re-recording, or by chemical reproduction, or by other equivalent techniques, which accurately reproduces the original.

Rule 1002; Requirement of Original

To prove the content of a writing, recording, or photograph, the original writing, recording, or photograph is required, except as otherwise provided in these rules or by statute.

Rule 1003; Admissibility of Duplicates

A duplicate is admissible to the same extent as an original unless (1) a genuine question is raised as to the authenticity of the original or (2) in the circumstances it would be unfair to admit the duplicate in lieu of the original.

Rule 1004; Admissibility of Other Evidence of Contents

The original is not required, and other evidence of the contents of a writing, recording, or photograph is admissible if–

(1) *Originals lost or destroyed*. All originals are lost or have been destroyed, unless the proponent lost or destroyed them in bad faith; or

(2) *Original not obtainable*. No original can be obtained by any available judicial process or procedure; or

(3) *Original in possession of opponent*. At a time when an original was under the control of the party against whom offered, that party was put on notice, by the pleadings or otherwise, that the contents would be a subject of proof at the hearing, and that party does not produce the original at the hearing; or

(4) *Collateral matters*. The writing, recording, or photograph is not closely related to a controlling issue.

Rule 1005; Public Records

The contents of an official record, or of a document authorized to be recorded or filed and actually recorded or filed, including data compilations in any form, if otherwise admissible, may be proved by copy, certified as correct in accordance with Rule 902 or testified to be correct by a witness who has compared it with the original. If a copy which complies with the foregoing cannot be obtained by the exercise of reasonable diligence, then other evidence of the contents may be given.

Rule 1006; Summaries

The contents of voluminous writings, recordings, or photographs which cannot conveniently be examined in court may be presented in the form of a chart, summary, or calculation. The originals, or duplicates, shall be made available for examination or copying, or both, by other parties at reasonable time and place. The court may order that they be produced in court.

Rule 1007; Testimony or Written Admission of a Party

Contents of writings, recordings, or photographs may be proved by the testimony or deposition of the party against whom offered or by that party's written admission, without accounting for the nonproduction of the original.

Rule 1008; Functions of Court and Jury

When the admissibility of other evidence of contents of writings, recordings, or photographs under these rules depends upon the fulfillment of a condition of fact, the question whether the condition has been fulfilled is ordinarily for the court to determine in accordance with the provisions of Rule 104. However, when an issue is raised (a) whether the asserted writing ever existed, or (b) whether another writing, recording, or photograph produced at the trial is the original, or (c) whether other evidence of contents correctly reflects the contents, the issue is for the trier of fact to determine as in the case of other issues of fact.

PART XI – Miscellaneous

Rule 1101; Applicability

(a) **Rules applicable.** Except as otherwise provided in subdivision (b), these rules apply to all actions and proceedings in the courts of this state.

(b) **Rules inapplicable.** The rules other than those with respect to privileges do not apply in the following situations and proceedings:

   (1) *Preliminary questions of fact.* The determination of questions of fact preliminary to admissibility of evidence when the issue is to be determined by the court under Rule 104(a).

   (2) *Grand jury.* Proceedings before grand juries.

   (3) *Miscellaneous proceedings.* Proceedings for extradition or rendition; sentencing, or granting or revoking probation; issuance of warrants for arrest, criminal summonses, and search warrants; and proceedings with respect to release on bail or otherwise.

   (4) *Contempt proceedings.* Contempt proceedings in which the court may act summarily.

   (5) *Small claims.* Small claims division of the district court.

   (6) *In camera custody hearings.* In camera proceedings in child custody matters to determine a child's custodial preference.

(7) *Proceedings involving juveniles.* Proceedings in the family division of the circuit court wherever MCR subchapter 3.900 states that the Michigan Rules of Evidence do not apply.

(8) *Preliminary examinations.* At preliminary examinations in criminal cases, hearsay is admissible to prove, with regard to property, the ownership, authority to use, value, possession and entry.

(9) *Domestic Relations Matters.* The court's consideration of a report or recommendation submitted by the friend of the court pursuant to MCL 552.505(1)(g) or (h).

(10) *Mental Health Hearings.* In hearings under Chapters 4, 4A, 5, and 6 of the Mental Health Code, MCL 330.1400 et seq., the court may consider hearsay data that are part of the basis for the opinion presented by a testifying mental health expert.

Rule 1102; Title

These rules are named the Michigan Rules of Evidence and may be cited as MRE. The notes following the individual rules were drafted by the chair and the reporter of the committee which drafted the proposed rules of evidence for the benefit of the bench and bar and are not authoritative constructions by the Court.

www.ingramcontent.com/pod-product-compliance
Lightning Source LLC
Chambersburg PA
CBHW071818170526
45167CB00003B/1351